C000066360

B'HEAD - 63
CHESTER - 7
WALLASEY - 37
CROSVILLE - 58
THAMESVALLEY - 25
OPEN ST 'CASE TDI

THE HEYDAY OF THE BUS
THE POSTWAR YEARS

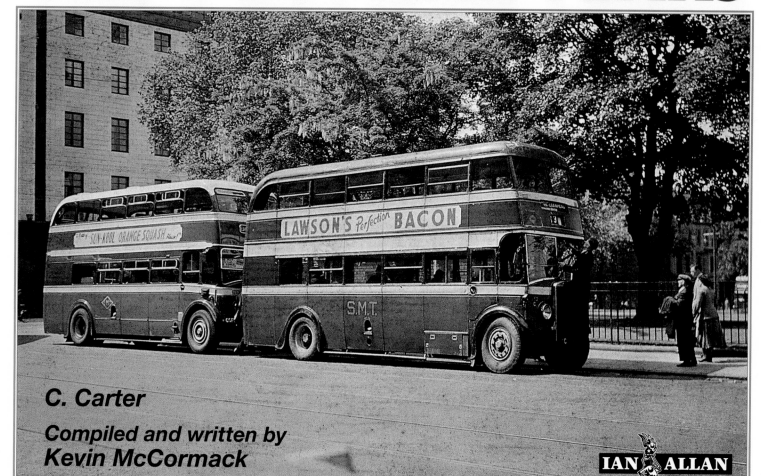

C. Carter

Compiled and written by
Kevin McCormack

IAN ALLAN Publishing

First published 1997

ISBN 0 7110 2514 2

© Kevin McCormack 1997

Published by Ian Allan Publishing

an imprint of Ian Allan Ltd, Terminal House, Station Approach, Shepperton, Surrey TW17 8AS.
Printed by Ian Allan Printing Ltd, Coombelands House, Coombelands Lane, Addlestone, Surrey KT15 1HY·

Code: 9704/B3

All photographs in this book by C. Carter

Front cover:
Full up inside
This Park Royal-bodied AEC Regent 1, dating from 1933, is bursting at the seams as it makes its way from Shoeburyness to Southend on 6 June 1949. Westcliff-on-Sea Motor Services was one of the few large operators not to use fleet numbers.

Back cover:
Buses on diversion
Chester Corporation placed an order for Metro-Cammell-bodied Daimler CVD6s in 1948 and then changed its mind. The buses went instead to Salford Corporation and No 343, the first of eight of these rather old-fashioned vehicles, is pictured at Bolton on 21 August 1949. The highlight of this vehicle's operational career was a visit to Copenhagen, in Denmark. Withdrawal came in 1963, followed by a sale to a showman.

Title page:
Out of the blue
The old livery of the Scottish Motor Traction Co was giving way to the familiar green and cream when this view was taken at St Andrew Square, Edinburgh, on 18 June 1951. Balancing on a dumb iron and the starting handle, the driver adjusts the blinds of 1938-built Leyland TD5 No J52. Parked up behind is a sleek 1949 Duple-bodied AEC Regent III, No BB62.

Left:
Facts of life
Storks carrying babies may be an image from the past, but so is Southdown Motor Services, which had served Sussex since 1915. Standing at Pool Valley bus station, Brighton, on 18 June 1949 is No 336, one of 80 Leyland PD2/1s built for Southdown in 1948/49. This vehicle was withdrawn in 1965.

Introduction

Here is another in the well-known 'Heyday' series of transport colour albums, but this one is rather different. All the photographs were taken within a three-year time span; not in itself remarkable, except that the period covered is 1949 to 1952, when colour photography was virtually unknown. Indeed, in the case of some of the older vehicles and liveries, the pictures in this book may be the only ones ever taken of them in colour. Even the newer buses, which remained in service up to the 1960s or later, have probably not been seen before in colour in their original condition.

What you see in these pages is pure nostalgia: peaceful days with no traffic, the boom years of public transport that followed World War 2, before private car ownership became widespread and television encouraged people to stay indoors. This really was the 'Heyday of the Bus'. The year 1949 witnessed the peak in new bus and coach registrations, and many operators obtained their best ever passenger loadings in this period. By 1952, however, the tide was beginning to turn, but that is another story.

Credit for having the foresight to take these historic photographs belongs to Mr C. Carter, who persevered with the primitive colour technology of the day whilst virtually every other transport photographer worked exclusively in monochrome. Carter, as he prefers to be known, has been a road transport photographer for most of his life, having 'caught the bug' from living near a tramway system as a child. Brought up in Leyton and then Buckhurst Hill, on the northeast outskirts of London, he can remember travelling on the last B-type buses, and the wonderful view which a small boy could obtain through the low windows, something which was not possible with the loftier, newer NS-type. Carter's first photograph was of a Southmet tram at Crystal Palace in 1933 and in the summer of 1939 he was given his first colour roll, a Dufay 120 film with eight exposures. One of these, a pair of London Transport LTs with

wartime markings, appears in *The Heyday of the London Bus — 3.*

Before Carter could obtain any more Dufay film, he was called up for the war, serving as a gunner and radio operator on Halifax bombers with No 614 Pathfinder Squadron in North Africa and Italy. Surviving unscathed, he re-entered 'civvy street' and spent the remainder of his working life as a manager in industry. He is now retired and lives with his wife and grown-up son in south London.

In the early postwar years, tramways were closing all over Britain and Carter started to record these in monochrome and Dufay colour, using an Ensign Selfix camera. He travelled widely, using public transport and staying in youth hostels. Before leaving a tramway (or trolleybus) system, he would usually take a token colour picture of a bus, not a predetermined one but anything at hand. What is reproduced in this book represents virtually his entire collection of bus transparencies from this early period, apart from his few London shots which have been featured in the companion volumes on buses in London.

Although other colour film existed before and immediately after the war (the American GIs stationed in Britain had access to Ektachrome), transport photographers started using colour in earnest only from the mid-1950s and much of the film exposed was devoted to capturing the last decade of steam on British Railways. Even then, by the mid-1960s, many films were still rated at only 25ASA, but that was fast compared to the 2ASA that Dufay offered! The best Carter could get was 1/50th of a second on an aperture of F4.5 in good sunlight. On a dull day it was almost impossible to hold the camera sufficiently steady to obtain a sharp photograph unless there was something to lean against. But Dufay gave good colours which have lasted well. The process involved pre-printing of inks onto the film and an image being formed by a *'réseau'* (web), which was a series of tiny dots similar to those on a television screen. However, this has meant that for publication the transparencies have had to be copied onto a modern film suitable for scanning. Consequently, there may be a very slight loss of colour and definition.

As well as being very slow, Dufay was also temperamental. Each film varied in colour and was supplied with a plastic filter to enhance or suppress the shades, as appropriate. The filter was meant to be fitted on the inside of the lens, but it was bad enough having to insert a new film, never mind a filter, into the camera after eight exposures, an operation which usually took place on the pavement. To make life easier, Carter made a cardboard frame for the filter and attached it to the outside of the camera around the lens. With all these technical difficulties, it is remarkable that Carter managed to produce such good results.

In these pages we see examples from all the major bus manufacturers of the period —

Leyland, AEC, Bristol, Daimler, Guy, Albion, Crossley, Bedford and Dennis. What is amazing is that only the last named is still making buses! Leyland and AEC dominated the market in the early postwar years with their PDs and Regents respectively. Fortunately, variety was obtained through operators specifying bodies from a wide range of builders.

As well as the changes that have occurred in the bus manufacturing industry over the years, the operating side has also seen dramatic developments since World War 2: nationalisation, mergers (still continuing), the creation (and dismantling) of bodies like the National Bus Company, Scottish Bus Group and the various Passenger Transport Executives, local government reorganisation, deregulation and privatisation. No attempt has been made to cover these aspects in this book apart from the occasional passing reference. In fact, captioning

has generally been kept fairly short to allow maximum coverage for the photographs.

In compiling and writing this book, I must express my gratitude to Mr Carter for allowing his material to be used and I also wish to thank Peter Waller of Ian Allan Ltd, Jeff Johnson and Bill Ballard for their assistance. I have used a variety of sources for the data in this book and I would like particularly to mention the excellent information published by the PSV Circle.

My aim has been to produce a fitting tribute to a pioneering colour photographer and I hope that readers will enjoy perusing this unique collection.

Kevin R. McCormack
Ashtead
Surrey
January 1997

Left:
Colour change
Newcastle Corporation's blue and white livery had given way to cadmium yellow, cream and maroon when No 106 was photographed at Newcastle Central station on 23 August 1952. This bus belonged to a batch of 22 AEC Regent IIIs with Massey bodies, delivered in 1948/49.

Right:
All change
Basking in the evening sunlight at Blackburn station terminus on 20 August 1949 is Ribble Motor Services No 2482, which was one of a batch of 38 Leyland PD1As built in 1947 with lowbridge Brush bodies. Although 16 were later sold, the remaining 22 were widened to 8ft and fitted with new Burlingham bodywork for further service.

Above:
Faithful servant
Apart from the addition of some rubber-mounted windows in 1959, this Beadle-bodied Bristol K5G, dating from 1949, looked much the same throughout its 19 years of service with Pontypridd Urban District Council. No 56 passes the Post Office in The Broadway, Pontypridd, on 11 June 1952.

Right:
Bus enthusiast
Chester was one of the first municipalities to replace all its trams with motorbuses. Pictured outside the cathedral on 6 May 1950 is No 45, a 1943 Daimler CWG5 ('W' standing for wartime) with a very lofty looking Massey-built Austerity body. The bus remained in service until 1954.

Right:

Long-distance traveller

Buses are well known for making a one-way journey to Wombwell, never to return, but here is a bus which used to make return journeys every day. Preparing for its five-hour marathon of nearly 40 miles from Leeds to Rawmarsh is a 1946-built AEC Regent II fitted with a very austere Strachan lowbridge body. No 53 belonged to T. Burrow &

Sons of Wombwell, whose operations were taken over by Yorkshire Traction in October 1966. When this view was taken at Leeds bus station on 27 August 1952, the vehicle was already halfway through its short working life. A Leeds Corporation tram can be seen in the background.

Left:
Off colour
This 1937-built AEC Regent was one of only a handful of Sheffield Corporation vehicles to be painted in an experimental green livery before reverting to the familiar blue and cream seen on the vehicles in the background. When photographed at Pond Street on 28 August 1952, No 356 had just received a new Roe body.

Right:
Howzat!
The famous cricketer, Denis Compton, peers through the cab of Sunderland District Omnibus Co No 224, a brand-new Roe-bodied AEC Regent III complete with London Transport-style rear-wheel discs. Caught on camera on 21 September 1950 at Sunderland station, this bus passed to Northern General in 1962 and, as No 2042, was withdrawn two years later.

Above:

Alexander the Great

For over three decades, until the company was divided up into separate businesses in 1961, W. Alexander & Sons of Falkirk grew to become Britain's third largest operator, with a fleet of some 2,000 vehicles. In addition, the company was also a builder of bus and coach bodies. Dundee, on 19 June 1951, finds RO 545, a Guy Arab II of 1945 vintage fitted with a Weymann-built Austerity lowbridge body. After transfer to Alexander (Midland), the vehicle was withdrawn in 1963.

Right:

Big builder

In the early postwar period, the battle for new bus orders was mainly between AEC and Leyland. AEC swallowed up Crossley, Maudslay and Park Royal and had a phenomenal production run of around 8,000 for its Regent III chassis. Admittedly, over half of these were London Transport RTs, but the type was also favoured by many provincial operators, such as Western Welsh, whose No 628 is seen at Pontypridd on 11 June 1952.

Left:

Hard times

Pity the people of Widnes in warm weather sitting on wooden benches in a bus with
only four opening windows! This wartime Duple-bodied Daimler CWD6, No 56 in the
corporation fleet, was photographed at Widnes town hall on 18 May 1950. Notice the
chequered kerb stones and a Belisha beacon which seems to have become separated
from the pedestrian crossing.

Above:

Enduring design

The style of Metro-Cammell bodywork carried on this Nottingham Corporation vehicle
originated in 1933 and was still being produced for this operator as late as 1949. No 24
was an AEC Regent II dating from 1939 which remained in service until 1957. On
20 August 1951 it is seen under the wires at Market Square, Nottingham, in sparkling
condition, complete with rolled-up radiator muff.

Left:
Catch that tiger
Caerphilly Urban District Council No 1, a Leyland Tiger PS2/5, should have carried a Bruce body but, due to that company's closure, it received one from Massey instead. Withdrawn in 1969, this vehicle was subsequently used as a trainer and towing vehicle, fortunately surviving long enough to be preserved. This is how it looked on 12 June 1952, when new, attracting some enthusiastic passengers in its home town.

Above:
In the line of duty
A row of Grimsby Corporation Guys and AECs stand ready for service on 22 August 1951. In the foreground is No 76, a Guy Arab II dating from 1944. Grimsby's fleet merged with that of neighbouring Cleethorpes in 1957.

Left:
Airbus
New to Yorkshire Traction in 1946, this Roe-bodied Leyland PD1, No 726, served as a control tower following withdrawal in 1961 before being rescued for preservation in 1980. On 19 September 1950 it was advertising Manchester in Doncaster.

Above:
Family tradition
Samuel Ledgard started a char-a-banc service in 1913 and went on to build up a thriving business in the Leeds and Bradford areas until he died in 1952. The executors of his estate then continued operations until 1967 when they sold out to West Yorkshire. In 1946 Ledgard had bought six Leyland PD1s, one of which, JUM 375, is seen here in Bradford on 22 September 1950.

17

Left:
Stop press
With his newspaper spread across the steering wheel, the driver takes a break from driving brand-new Darwen Corporation No 39 in Blackburn on 21 August 1949. The vehicle was one of a batch of 10 Crossley DD42/7s and remained in service until 1964. A decade later, in April 1974, Blackburn Corporation took over Darwen's operations following the local government reorganisation of that year.

Above:
Small time operator
Another new bus takes to the road, this time in the ownership of a municipality which, for many years, had the smallest fleet, with only three vehicles (and these were all destroyed by fire in 1943). Bedwas & Machen Urban District Council No 8, an AEC Regent III with Northern Counties bodywork, was photographed in Caerphilly on 12 June 1952.

Above:

Out of work

Homegoing factory workers at Bishop's Stortford wait patiently to board Hicks Bros No 76, a Strachan-bodied Guy Arab II, on 1 August 1949. In the following year, this Braintree-based operator was acquired by Eastern National and the vehicle was renumbered EN1186.

Left:
Food for thought

James Bullock of Featherstone started out in business as a greengrocer before recognising the commercial potential of the developing public transport industry. By the time J. Bullock & Sons (1928) Ltd, operating as the B&S Motor Service, sold out to the West Riding Automobile Co in September 1950, it had a fleet of 170 vehicles including No 294, one of six AEC Regent IIIs with Roe lowbridge bodies built in 1947. On 27 August 1952 No 294 still proudly carried its former owner's distinctive livery when seen in Leeds. The vehicle remained in service until 1962.

Right:
Rise and fall

West Hartlepool Corporation No 67, one of 15 Leyland PD2/3s delivered to the corporation in 1950, waits in Church Street on 24 August 1951. It was in this year that Leyland acquired Albion; it would later also capture AEC, Guy and Daimler. Who could then have predicted the ultimate demise of the all-conquering Leyland company?

Left:

Prewar legacy

With its splendid lettering and distinctly 1930s shape, this Metro-Cammell-bodied Daimler CVG6 ('V' for victory) hardly fits the image of a bus built in 1948. Still looking as good as new, West Bromwich Corporation No 144 rests at Wolverhampton on 10 July 1949.

Above:

Artistic licence

Luton Corporation's policy of painting registration numbers and advertisements directly onto its buses is demonstrated on Leyland PD2/1 No 121 and Crossley DD42 No 100, both of which were lowbridge vehicles dating from 1948. Unfortunately, the attractive livery seen here on 21 May 1949 was later changed to an uninspiring dull red. In 1970 the corporation sold out to United Counties but this was too late for Nos 121 and 100, which had been withdrawn in 1968 and 1965 respectively.

Above:
Go faster livery
Memories of the prewar streamline era are evoked by the colour scheme adopted by Kingston-upon-Hull Corporation for its bus fleet and displayed by No 304 at Hull bus station on 23 August 1951. This vehicle was one a class of 56 AEC Regent IIIs with Weymann bodies built in 1949. It remained in service until 1968.

Right:
Stairway to heaven
Four months after being photographed at Reading (General) station on 4 June 1949, this veteran, one of the last open-staircase buses to run in normal service in Britain, was heading for the great garage in the sky. Thames Valley Traction Co No 170 was a Leyland Titan TD1, which originally entered service in June 1928. The company merged with Aldershot & District in 1972 to become Alder Valley.

THAMES·VALLEY

Left:

Sign of the times

The nationalisation in the late 1940s of certain major bus operators — the Tilling Group, SMT and London Transport — was seen as a threat by many independent operators, such as City, which had been forced to surrender its routes in the capital in 1934. Brave words are written on the bus, but to no avail, for City succumbed to the nationalised Eastern National in 1952. Three years earlier, on 3 June 1949, new lowbridge Daimler CVD6, No D2, calls at Gants Hill *en route* from London (Wood Green) to Southend.

Above:

Gothic revival

East Yorkshire Motor Services was renowned for its domed-roof double-deckers designed to fit through the 15th century North Bar at Beverley. This view at Hull bus station on 23 August 1951 features Guy Arab No 411, which was fitted with Utility bodywork by Charles H. Roe of Crossgates, near Leeds.

Left:
Aerial view
Television was still in its infancy in the early 1950s and rooftop antennae were not a common sight (particularly growing out of chimney pots!). Featured in this drab scene in Milford Street on 14 June 1952 is Swindon Corporation No 77, a Daimler CVG6 built in 1947 with Park Royal bodywork.

Above:
Clocking-off time
The workers of Bury queue for a seat on Ramsbottom Corporation No 15. This Roe-bodied Leyland TS7, built as recently as 1937 despite its ancient appearance, was recorded on 20 May 1950.

29

Above:
No traffic wardens
In the early postwar period, the only double yellow lines in Dundee were on the buses. There was plenty to keep the corporation painters busy on vehicles like this 1949 Daimler CVD6 seen on 19 June 1951.

Right:
Hunting in pairs
These two AEC Regents belonging to West Bridgford Urban District Council have ventured into the territory of the council's larger neighbour, Nottingham Corporation. Nottingham was eventually to end West Bridgford's 56 years of independent operation, taking over services in 1972. West Bridgford No 4, depicted on 20 August 1951, has Park Royal highbridge bodywork and dates from 1939. In 1953 it received a Willowbrook lowbridge body and was withdrawn in 1965.

Above:

Any old iron

Standing alongside these ornate railings, which escaped being melted down for the war effort, is a line-up of Central SMT Leylands. No L253 has Leyland lowbridge bodywork and remained in service until 1962. Behind is No L236, which survived until 1965, having been sold to Scottish Omnibuses of Edinburgh. This view was taken on 22 June 1951 in Carlton Place, Glasgow.

Right:

High and mighty

Eastern National Bristol GO5G No 3654, dating from 1937, proudly displays its new Eastern Coachworks bodywork at Southend (Victoria) station on 22 July 1950, having discarded its previous Brush-built body. Eastern National, which originated in 1929 following the splitting of the former National Steam Car Co, was taken over by Thomas Tilling in 1931 and nationalised in 1948.

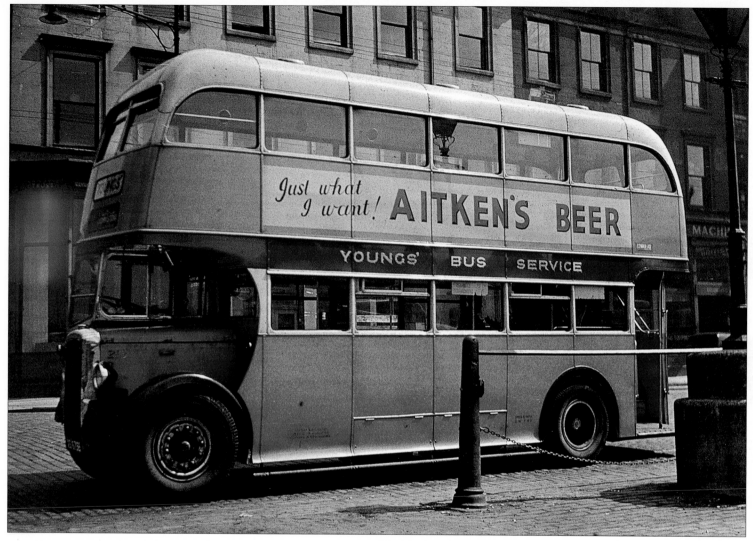

Left:

Under attack

The harmful effects of sea air are readily apparent on the window frames of this two-year-old Weymann-bodied AEC Regent III pictured at Aberdeen railway station on 26 June 1951. The corporation's bold lettering on this bus renders further identification unnecessary.

Above:

Showing its true colours

The distinctive livery of Youngs of Paisley lived on for a while following its take-over by Western SMT. A total of 109 buses were transferred to the new owner, including this Daimler CVG6, which was photographed in Glasgow on 22 June 1951. Youngs bought six of these Northern Counties-bodied vehicles in 1949; this example became No 2213 with Western SMT, lasting in service until 1964.

Above:

Municipal survivor

Warrington Corporation is one of the few local authorities still operating buses at the time of writing, but, alas, not Bristol K6Gs like No 49 seen here amid a rare display of other traffic in its home town on 18 May 1950. This attractive vehicle, fitted with Bruce bodywork, remained in service until 1963.

Right:

Change of direction

The style of livery, together with the mechanical semaphore indicators, conveys a somewhat dated image of Wallasey Corporation and yet only eight years later the municipality was pioneering the operation of rear-engined Leyland Atlanteans. Leaving Birkenhead (Woodside) station on 15 May 1950 is No 15, a Leyland PD1 with Metro-Cammell highbridge bodywork. In 1953, the bus received a replacement Willowbrook body, which extended the vehicle's operational life to 1965.

37

Left:
Past its sell-by date
If this photograph at Doncaster, taken on 19 September 1950, had been taken a few months earlier, we would have seen this Lincolnshire Road Car Co AEC in the livery of its previous owner, Enterprise & Silver Dawn Motors of Scunthorpe. No 820 was one of five such Regent IIs built with Burlingham bodies which were replaced in 1956 by Roe bodies dating from 1948/49. Lincolnshire Road Car became part of Yorkshire Traction's expanding empire in 1988.

Above:
Regal at the Gaumont
These names conjure up rival cinemas, but the Regal was also the AEC single-decker much favoured by City of Oxford Motor Services, which bought 29 of these Willowbrook-bodied vehicles in 1949/50. Pulling out from behind No 722 is Bristol K6A No L4119, which was fitted with Eastern Coachworks lowbridge bodywork. The location is Swindon and the date is 14 June 1952.

39

Above:

Prize exhibit

During the Festival of Britain, bus operators took turns at presenting their latest vehicles. On 3 June 1951, Southdown Motor Services showed the first of a class of 76 Leyland Titan PD2/12s, a vehicle which ran until 1970. On the South Bank, in the shadow of the viaduct leading into Charing Cross station, No 701 shares a plinth with a street light display.

Right:

Pow-wow

Under the gaze of the Red Indian radiator mascot, the crew of this Guy Arab III, disguised as warehouse keepers, chat at Sunderland station on 21 September 1950. Northern General was another exponent of intricate lining, but quickly lost interest in No 1236, which was scrapped in 1960 after only 11 years in service.

41

Left:

Hit the roof

This was probably the reaction at the Benfleet & District garage to the damage sustained by this otherwise smart Park Royal-bodied 1945 Daimler CWA6, pictured at South Benfleet on 22 July 1950. FOP 462 was formerly Birmingham City Transport No 1462 and, appropriately perhaps, was converted to open-top condition after acquisition by Southend Corporation in 1955. The vehicle survived until 1970, but Benfleet & District lasted only until 1951, when it was absorbed by Eastern National.

Above:

Vision of the future

Full-fronted vehicles with radiator grilles were starting to come into fashion in the early postwar years. Indeed, 1948-built Blackpool Corporation No 212, one of a batch of 100 Leyland PD2/5s with Burlingham bodywork, follows a prewar design reminiscent of the trams from that period, some of which are still in use today. On the other hand, Lytham St Annes No 18, dating from 1947, is a Leyland PD1 of traditional appearance. This view was taken at Blackpool Central station on 19 May 1950.

Left:

Unlucky triplet

No 63 was one of three Leyland TD4c buses with English Electric bodywork delivered to Preston Corporation in 1936. Photographed on 29 May 1950, this one had the shortest life of the trio, being withdrawn in 1953.

Right:

Re-chassied

In contrast with the more usual practice of rebodying, Maidstone & District No 280, seen here at Maidstone's Lower Stone Street bus station on 18 March 1950, has received a new chassis. The Weymann lowbridge body dates from 1936 and was originally fitted to a Bristol GO5G, but the whole batch of chassis was returned to the manufacturers in 1939 and ended up in Bath (see page 48). In exchange, M&D received new K5G chassis, on which the Weymann bodies were remounted. On the left is M&D No 176, a Weymann-bodied Bristol K6A dating from 1947.

Left:

Life extension

Many prewar vehicles were disguised as modern buses by the fitting of new bodies, which had the effect of extending their operational careers and saving costs. A typical example was this Leyland TD4 of East Midland, No D12, depicted at Waterdale, Doncaster on 19 September 1950 with new Willowbrook bodywork. The brown, yellow and cream livery preceded the more familiar red.

Above:

Breaking the code

No C1247 in the fleet of Chepstow-based operator Red & White Services Ltd was quite simply the 12th coach delivered in 1947. This Duple-bodied Albion CX13, pictured at Cardiff on 11 June 1952, ran until 1962. Red & White commenced operations in 1930 and was, at the time of its nationalisation in 1950, the largest independent operator in Britain, with a fleet of 380 vehicles.

Right:

Urban decay

Contrasting with the backdrop of war-damaged Sheffield, is a brand-new Weymann-bodied Guy Arab III, No 180 in the fleet of Chesterfield Corporation and one of 20 such vehicles. The photograph was taken on 20 September 1950.

Left:

No offence

Parking next to a pedestrian crossing is now illegal, but no such restrictions applied on 13 June 1952 when Bath Electric Tramways No 3814 was photographed. This vehicle has one of the 16 Bristol GO5G chassis dating from 1936/37 which were disposed of by Maidstone & District in 1939 (see page 45). Originally rebodied by Bristol, No 3814 had acquired an Eastern Coachworks body by the date of this view. Bath Electric Tramways was taken over by the Bristol Omnibus Co in 1970.

Above:

Contrasting styles

Hope Street, Wigan, on 18 May 1950 finds two lowbridge AEC Regent IIIs of similar vintage (1948/49) but fitted with different bodies. The Leigh Corporation vehicle, from a batch of 12 numbered 25-36, has Roberts bodywork, whereas St Helens Corporation No C30, one of eight in the class, is fitted with an East Lancs body. The St Helens vehicles ran for only 10 years, but Leigh's lasted well into the 1960s.

Above:

Doubtful parentage

This strange vehicle with the sad radiator is a 1935 Dennis Lance, one of six delivered to Thomas Tilling just prior to that company's South Coast operations passing to Brighton, Hove & District, in whose fleet it became No 6313. Converted in 1949 to open-top and disguised as an AEC, the Dennis was transferred to Westcliff-on-Sea Motors and is seen here on the seafront at Southend on 22 July 1950.

Right:

Air Despatch

This was the unusual name of the body manufacturer of Cardiff Corporation No 96, one of 10 AEC Regent IIs delivered in 1947. Photographed on 11 June 1952, No 96 was fitted with rubber-mounted windows in 1961 and withdrawn in 1964. Air Despatch of Pengam Airport, Cardiff, changed its name to the more familiar Bruce Coachworks.

Above:
Old Firm
This Wroughton-based operator uses a 1944 Duple-bodied Bedford wartime Utility OWB to attract a customer in Swindon on 14 June 1952. It is probably no coincidence that the livery resembles that of Swindon Corporation.

Right:
Hereditary title
From the prewar Dennis Lance seen overleaf to the early postwar version, a 1949 K2 with Weymann lowbridge body. No 416 in the Lancashire United fleet was photographed on 18 May 1950, before the attractive livery gave way to a more mundane all-over red. Remarkably, the Dennis Lance is still being made, but today it is as a rear-engined single-deck chassis.

Left:
Name dropper
Pictured at Wigan bus station on 18 May 1950 is another elaborately liveried bus, in this case one which is about to lose its Titan badge on the radiator. No 115 belonged to a batch of 14 lowbridge Leyland TD7s delivered to Wigan Corporation in 1940. Wartime restrictions introduced after the batch's construction would soon banish refinements like the draught excluders fitted to the tops of the windows.

Above:
Bristol fashion
No 3629 in the Bristol Tramways fleet looks in excellent shape for its age, although it has only four more years to run. Originally a Park Royal-bodied product from 1942, the Bristol K5G had only recently been rebodied when photographed in Bristol on 14 June 1952. Its 'new' body is in fact older than its chassis, having originally been fitted to vehicle No C3173 in 1938.

55

Left:
Doorstep delivery
This house in Caerphilly receives personal service in the shape of local corporation No 21, a 1945-built Guy Arab II with Roe lowbridge bodywork. Fitted in 1957 with rubber-mounted windows, No 21 lasted until 1967. It is seen here on 12 June 1952.

Above:
Madder and white
This was the official description of Edinburgh Corporation's famous livery, which is still perpetuated by Lothian Regional Transport today. Edinburgh was not normally associated with AECs, but seven Regent IIIs with Brockhouse bodies were purchased in 1950. These included No G236 seen here on 18 June 1951. This bus was withdrawn in 1960.

Left:
Sorry state
Contrasting with the smart appearance of most of the buses featured in this book is Crosville Motor Services No MB257, which was only two years old when photographed at Liverpool's Pier Head on 15 June 1950. This type of bodywork had a tendency to warp and in 1958 the vehicle received a replacement body dating from 1950. Renumbered DKA257, it was withdrawn from service in 1961.

Above right:
Moving scene
Using a slow Dufay film on a dull day has almost turned these Leeds shoppers into sprinters. The photograph, taken at the bus station on 27 August 1952, features GWX 823, a Kippax & District Leyland PD2/1 built in 1948. In June 1956 it came into the ownership of Wallace Arnold, the well-known coach operator, which took over Kippax & District. The bus remained in service until 1967.

Right:
Tough guy
This bulky Guy Arab III was one of 26 eight-footers with Northern Coachbuilders bodywork delivered to the Gateshead & District Omnibus Co. Seen in Newcastle on 23 August 1952, No 23 became Northern General No 45 in 1960 and remained in service until 1963. By this time Guy had been taken over by Jaguar. The latter was in turn to be acquired by Leyland, thereby bringing about the demise of another famous bus manufacturer.

Above:

High street bus-tle

This view at Swindon on 14 June 1952 recaptures busy shopping days when the only traffic seemed to be buses. The absence of parked cars allows a clear run for this 1944 Strachan-bodied Guy Arab II which, after rebodying by Weymann, lasted until 1962.

Right:

Bolton wanderer

It's back to 21 August 1949 to record another new bus, a vehicle which was to survive long enough to be taken over by the newly created SELNEC PTE some 20 years later. Waiting at the Trinity Street terminus is Bolton Corporation No 427, one of a class of 100 Leyland PD2/4s. This vehicle was to become Oldham Corporation No 472 in 1966.

Left:
Blind fold
When Eastern Counties acquired this veteran Leyland Titan TD1 in 1945, the new owner made it look even older by abandoning the internal destination display. Instead the bus was fitted with the company's own tin-plate hinged design which operated like an upturned book, and was illuminated by ugly, protruding lights. The vehicle itself was new to Plymouth Corporation in 1930 (as No 121). It became Eastern Counties No A245 and is pictured entering Ipswich on 7 August 1950, its penultimate year of service.

Above:
Transport extravaganza
Birkenhead Woodside used to provide three means of transport and still does. Although the trains have vanished underground following the closure of the former LMS/GWR joint station, trams have arrived. But gone are Birkenhead Corporation's buses, with their distinctive Massey bodies and attractive blue livery; the latter lasted until Merseyside PTE took over in 1969. This Leyland Titan still carried the elaborate style of lettering when photographed on 15 May 1950.

Above:

Plenty of time

There is an unhurried atmosphere in this photograph as Middlesbrough Corporation No 44 stands beneath the church clock at North Ormesby on 25 August 1952. This Roe-bodied Leyland PD1, one of a trio supplied in 1946, was withdrawn by the corporation in 1956 and, after several changes of ownership, went for scrap in 1964.

Right:

Geography lesson

This Reading bus seen in Portsmouth on 16 August 1952 is not badly off course — it is just a 1947 Leyland PD1A of Portsmouth Corporation with bodywork supplied by a local builder which shared its name with the Berkshire town. Despite its rather old-fashioned and small (52-seat) body, No 199 ran until 1963.

Left:
Buried
Rochdale Corporation No 39, a 1948 AEC Regent III with Weymann bodywork, stands at Bury on 20 May 1950. The bus station and flowerbeds beyond have now disappeared under the Bury Interchange.

Above:
Spot the difference
On the same wet day, this time in Rawtenstall, two corporation Leyland PD2s display the slight variations in body styling which reflect the different ages of the vehicles. No 41, on the left, was built in 1947 and withdrawn in 1968. Nearer the camera, No 3 dates from 1949 and was transferred to Rossendale Joint Transport Committee in 1968, when Rawtenstall merged with Haslingden.

Left:
Singleminded
The Venture Transport Co (Newcastle) Ltd's fleet consisted entirely of single-deckers due to the proliferation of low bridges in its operating area. A total of 60 Daimler CVD6s with Willowbrook bodies were delivered in 1947 and No 139, seen here negotiating the streets of Newcastle on 23 August 1952, lasted until 1961.

Above:
Home-made
In 1947, Birch Brothers put into service seven Leyland PD1s with distinctive front-entrance bodies manufactured in the company's own workshops in Kentish Town. The vehicles were used on the operator's long-established route from Rushden and Bedford to King's Cross, where No K183 was photographed on 2 July 1950. Sadly, after only 10 years, the stylish coachwork was replaced by a box-shaped Weymann Orion body. Birch was another opponent of nationalisation, having lost 30 buses to London Transport back in 1934.

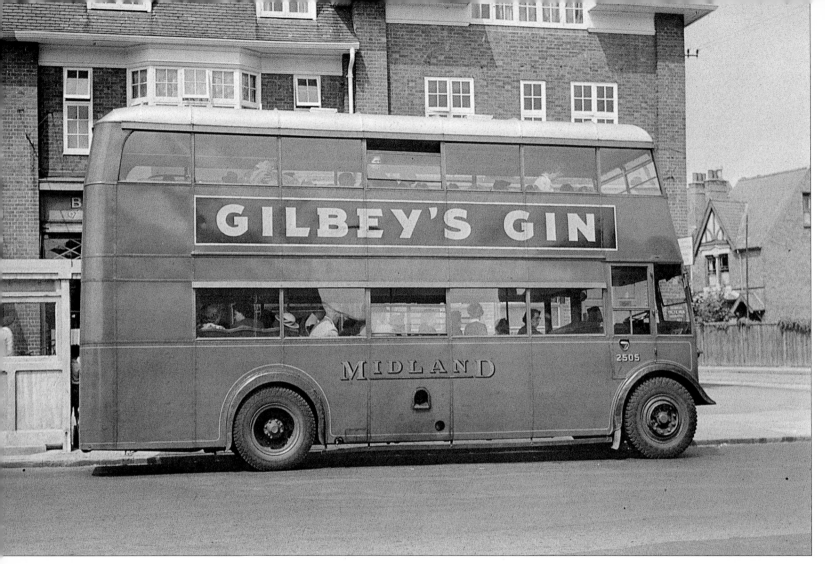

Above:

Provincial giant

The Birmingham & Midland Motor Omnibus Co Ltd ('BMMO'), trading as Midland Red, was not only the largest fleet operator outside London but, from 1923 to 1970, built its own buses. Only during the war years did BMMO take other makes such as this 1943-built Weymann-bodied Guy Arab II. Photographed on 9 July 1949 at Erdington, No 2505 ran until 1956.

Right:

Classic thoroughbred

As well as manufacturing chassis and engines, Leyland also built bus bodies, at least up until 1954. Several all-Leyland TDs and PDs feature in this book, a typical example being Accrington Corporation's PD2/1 No 111, which was photographed on 20 May 1950. One of seven delivered to the municipality in 1947, this vehicle served for 13 years and was eventually scrapped in 1966.

Left:
Lincoln green
No need to look for a London Transport RT. This photograph, taken on 22 August 1951, shows a real Lincoln green bus, a 1936 Leyland TD4. No 44 in the City Transport fleet, it remained in service until 1952. Lincoln's municipal operator was acquired by Yorkshire Traction in 1993 and is now part of the Lincolnshire Road Car operation.

Above:
Arch enemy
The viaduct serves as a reminder that railway and bus companies were for the most part rivals even if the degree of animosity portrayed in the contemporary Ealing comedy film *The Titfield Thunderbolt* was a slight exaggeration. In this view taken at Adelphi Street, Glasgow, on 22 June 1951, we see Western SMT No MD141, the last of a batch of 20 Leyland TD5s delivered in 1939.

73

Left:
Supporting role
Yorkshire Woollen District Transport No 545 acts as a convenient writing desk in this view at Leeds on 22 September 1950. One of nine Brush-bodied Leyland PD2/1s built in 1948 for Yorkshire, No 545 was sold in 1959 to AA Motor Services and was dismantled for spares the following year.

Above:
Ladies in waiting
Bedwas & Machen No 6 has some potential customers at Caerphilly on 12 June 1952. This handsome AEC Regal III with Bruce bodywork was the first of a pair delivered in 1951 and has been fitted with roof-mounted advertising boards. No 6 was withdrawn in 1967, but its twin, No 7, lives on in preservation.

Above:

Doncaster duo

Two corporation double-deckers with Roe bodies stand in their home town on 19 September 1950. They are No 58, an AEC Regent II dating from 1941, and No 55, a Leyland Titan TD5 built in 1939. The business of Charles H. Roe was taken over by Park Royal Vehicles in 1947, which in turn became part of the AEC empire two years later.

Right:

Stranger in the camp

This is no Scout jamboree, because that company's lowbridge Leyland PD2, No S9, stands alone among a large gathering of Ribble buses. These are mainly Burlingham-bodied Leylands, distinguished by their swept-back rear mudguards which have caught the sunlight. The scene is Tithebarn Street bus station in Preston on 19 May 1950. Scout eventually surrendered its independence to Ribble in 1961, although the livery was retained for a period thereafter. The famous Tithebarn Street terminus is now just a memory.

Above:

Wrong image

Although operators were all too grateful to receive Austerity buses in the mid-1940s to augment their war-damaged fleets, vehicles like this Northern Counties-bodied Guy Arab II looked dated for the 1950s compared with the designs then available. Middlesbrough Corporation No 17, pictured on 14 August 1949, was delivered in 1945 and withdrawn from service after only 10 years.

Right:

Popular choice

The rear-engined, front-entrance bus was yet to come and, although vehicles with full fronts and covered radiators were available in the early 1950s, many operators preferred the more traditional looking product. Typical was Rhondda Transport, which bought 33 AEC Regent IIIs with Weymann bodies in 1952. One of these was No 270, seen here in Sardis Road, Pontypridd, on 11 June 1952.

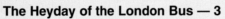